Floral TOUCHES

It's always the perfect time...

...to curl up with the **cheery comfort** of a floral afghan. With this set of five blossom-strewn designs to crochet, you can enjoy flowers year-round!

Each is **a celebration** of gardens or garden features. Just for fun, you can make a simple change of yarn color to turn the poinsettias of Winter Park into a blanket of early spring clematis.

In fact, why not experiment with color to make your afghans bloom in the hues and shades you like best? **Add a little more sunshine** to your day with these sweet indulgences!

LEISURE ARTS, INC.
Little Rock, Arkansas

I0894098

Rose PROMENADE

INTERMEDIATE

Finished Size: 48" x 66" (122 cm x 167.5 cm)

MATERIALS

Medium Weight Yarn MEDIUM 4
[6 ounces, 312 yards
(170 grams, 285 meters) per skein]:
Off-White - 7 skeins
Rose - 2 skeins
Green - 1 skein
Crochet hook, size J (6 mm) **or** size needed for gauge

GAUGE SWATCH: 9" (23 cm) square
Work same as Square.

STITCH GUIDE

TREBLE CROCHET ***(abbreviated tr)***
YO twice, insert hook in st or sp indicated, YO and pull up a loop (4 loops on hook), (YO and draw through 2 loops on hook) 3 times.

CLUSTER (uses one ch)
YO twice, insert hook in ch indicated, YO and pull up a loop, (YO and draw through 2 loops on hook) twice, YO 3 times, insert hook in same ch, YO and pull up a loop, (YO and draw through 2 loops on hook) 3 times, YO and draw through all 3 loops on hook.

FLOWER STRIP (Make 35)

With Rose and working in top 2 loops of chs ***(Fig. B, page 14)***, ch 8, slip st in fifth ch from hook **(petal made)**, ch 5, slip st in fifth ch from hook **(petal made)**, place marker around one petal to mark **right** side and bottom of Flower Strip, ★ ch 10, slip st in fifth ch from hook **(petal made)**, place marker in last ch worked into, ch 5, slip st in fifth ch from hook **(petal made)**; repeat from ★ 3 times **more**, (ch 5, slip st in fifth ch from hook) 3 times, place marker around third petal from hook to mark first joining, working across opposite side of Strip, † slip st in next marked ch, remove marker, ch 2, skip next 2 chs, slip st in next ch, ch 2, skip next ch, slip st in next ch, (ch 5, slip st in fifth ch from hook) twice †; repeat from † to † 3 times **more**, slip st in same ch as first slip st, ch 2, skip next 2 chs, slip st in last ch; finish off: 5 Flowers.

LEAF STRIP (Make 70)

With Green, ★ ch 6, work Cluster in fourth ch from hook **(Leaf made)**; repeat from ★ 4 times **more**, ch 1, place marker in ch just made for st placement; finish off: 5 Leaves.

SQUARE (Make 35)

With Off-White, ch 32; place marker in third ch from hook for st placement.

Row 1 (Right side)**:** Hdc in third ch from hook **(2 skipped chs count as first hdc)** and in each ch across; finish off: 31 hdc.

Note: Loop a short piece of yarn around any stitch on Row 1 to mark **right** side.

Instructions continued on page 4.

Row 2: With **right** side facing and working in Back Loops Only ***(Fig. 2a, page 26)***, join Rose with hdc in first hdc ***(see Joining With Hdc, page 26)***; hdc in next hdc and in each hdc across; finish off.

Row 3: With **wrong** side facing and working in horizontal bar only of each hdc ***(Fig. A)***, join Off-White with sc in first hdc ***(see Joining With Sc, page 26)***; sc in next hdc and in each hdc across, do **not** finish off.

Fig. A

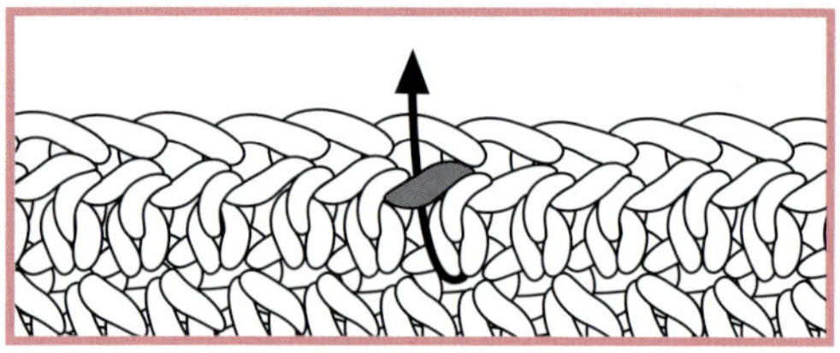

Row 4: Ch 2 **(counts as first dc, now and throughout)**, turn; working in Back Loops Only, dc in next sc, skip next sc, (dc, ch 1, dc) in next sc, ★ skip next sc, dc in next sc, skip next sc, (dc, ch 1, dc) in next sc; repeat from ★ across to last 3 sc, skip next sc, dc in last 2 sc: 24 dc and 7 ch-1 sps.

Row 5: Ch 2, turn; working in both loops, (dc, ch 1, dc) in next dc, skip next dc, dc in next ch-1 sp, ★ skip next dc, (dc, ch 1, dc) in next dc, skip next dc, dc in next ch-1 sp; repeat from ★ across to last 3 dc, skip next dc, dc in last 2 dc.

Row 6: Ch 2, turn; dc in Back Loop Only of next dc and each st across; finish off: 31 dc.

Row 7 (Joining row)**:** With **right** side of Square and Leaf Strip facing, join Off-White with slip st by inserting hook in marked ch on Leaf Strip **and** in first dc on Square; ch 2, remove marker, working **behind** Leaf Strip and in both loops of dc on Square only, dc in next 5 dc, ★ working **around** chs between Leaves, dc in next dc, working **behind** Leaf Strip **and** in both loops in dc on Square only, dc in next 5 dc; repeat from ★ 3 times **more**, skip next ch on Leaf Strip, dc in last ch of Leaf Strip **and** in last dc; do **not** finish off.

Row 8: Ch 2, turn; dc in Back Loop Only of next dc and each dc across.

Row 9: Ch 1, turn; sc in Front Loop Only of each dc across; finish off.

Row 10: With **right** side of Flower Strip and Square facing, join Off-White with slip st by inserting hook in center ch of marked petal on last Flower **and** in both loops of first sc on Square, ch 2, working **behind** Flower Strip and in both loops of sc on Square only, dc in next 5 sc, ★ working **around** Strip between Flowers, dc in next sc, working **behind** Flower Strip and in both loops of sc on Square only, dc in next 5 sc; repeat from ★ 3 times **more**, dc in last ch worked into on Flower Strip **and** in last sc on Square; do **not** finish off.

Rows 11 and 12: Repeat Rows 8 and 9.

Row 13: Repeat Row 7.

Row 14: Ch 1, turn; sc in Back Loop Only of each dc across.

Rows 15 and 16: Repeat Rows 4 and 5.

Finish off.

Row 17: With **right** side facing and working in Back Loops Only, join Rose with hdc in first dc; hdc in next dc and in each st across; finish off: 31 hdc.

Row 18: With **wrong** side facing and working in horizontal bar only of each hdc, join Off-White with sc in first hdc; sc in next hdc and in each hdc across; do **not** finish off.

Row 19: Ch 1, turn; sc in Front Loop Only of each sc across; finish off.

ASSEMBLY

Using Diagram as a guide for placement and being careful to have the beginning chains (BC) in the direction as shown on Diagram, join Squares into 5 vertical strips of 7 squares each, using Joining A and B; then join strips in same manner.

Placement Diagram

JOINING A

Join end of rows to free loops of beginning chs ***(Fig. 3b, page 26)*** as follows:

Place two Squares side-by-side with **right** sides facing. Keeping Off-White to **wrong** side throughout, insert hook in marked ch on **previous Square**, YO and pull up a loop, slip st in first row on **new Square**, slip st in next ch on **previous Square**, slip st in next row on **new Square**, skip next ch on **previous Square**, slip st in next ch, skip next row on **new Square**, slip st in next row, skip next ch on **previous Square**, slip st in next ch, † slip st in next row on **new Square**, skip next ch on **previous Square**, slip st in next ch †; repeat from † to † 3 times **more**, skip next row on **new Square**, slip st in next row, skip next ch on **previous Square**, slip st in next ch, repeat from † to † 6 times, skip next row on **new Square**, slip st in next row, skip next ch on **previous Square**, slip st in next ch, slip st in last row on **new Square**, slip st in last ch on **previous Square**; finish off.

JOINING B

Join sc to end of rows as follows:

Place two Squares side by side with **right** sides facing. Keeping Off-White to **wrong** side throughout, insert hook in first row on **previous Square**, YO and pull up a loop, slip st in first sc on **new Square**, slip st in next row on **previous Square**, skip next sc on **new Square**, slip st in next sc, skip next row on **previous Square**, slip st in next row, skip next sc on **new Square**, slip st in next sc, † slip st in next row on **previous Square**, skip next sc on **new Square**, slip st in next sc †; repeat from † to † 3 times **more**, skip next row on **previous Square**, slip st in next row, skip next sc on **new Square**, slip st in next sc, repeat from † to † 6 times, skip next row on **previous Square**, slip st in next row, skip next sc on **new Square**, slip st in next sc, slip st in last row on **previous Square**, slip st in last sc on **new Square**; finish off.

EDGING

Rnd 1: With **right** side facing, join Off-White with sc in sc at Point A on Diagram; † work 154 sc evenly spaced across, 2 sc in corner, work 214 sc evenly spaced across †, 2 sc in corner, repeat from † to † once, sc in same st as first sc; join with slip st to first sc: 744 sc.

Rnd 2: Working in Back Loops Only, slip st in next sc, ch 4 **(counts as first dc plus ch 1, now and throughout)**, dc in same st, ★ † [skip next sc, dc in next sc, skip next sc, (dc, ch 1, dc) in next sc] across to within one sc of next corner 2-sc group, skip next sc, (dc, ch 1, 2 dc, ch 1, dc) in next sc, skip next sc †, (dc, ch 1, dc) in next sc; repeat from ★ 2 times **more**, then repeat from † to † once; join with slip st to first dc: 570 dc and 194 ch-1 sps.

Rnd 3: Turn; (slip st, ch 4, dc) in next dc, ★ † skip next ch-1 sp, (dc, ch 1, tr) in next dc, ch 1, (tr, ch 1, dc) in next dc, skip next ch-1 sp, [(dc, ch 1, dc) in next dc, skip next dc, dc in next ch-1 sp, skip next dc] across to next corner group †, (dc, ch 1, dc) in next dc; repeat from ★ 2 times **more**, then repeat from † to † once; join with slip st to first dc, finish off.

Christmas BOUQUET

INTERMEDIATE

Finished Size: 39" x 58" (99 cm x 147.5 cm)

MATERIALS

Medium Weight Yarn
[7 ounces, 364 yards
(198 grams, 333 meters) per skein]:
- Off-White - 3 skeins
- Red - 1 skein
- Green - 1 skein
- Yellow - 1 skein

Crochet hook, size J (6 mm) **or** size needed for gauge
Safety pin
Yarn needle

GAUGE SWATCH: 7½" (19 cm) from straight edge to straight edge
Work same as Motif A.

STITCH GUIDE

TREBLE CROCHET *(abbreviated tr)*
YO twice, insert hook in st or sp indicated, YO and pull up a loop (4 loops on hook), (YO and draw through 2 loops on hook) 3 times.

LEAF (uses next 3 dc)
★ YO twice, insert hook in **next** dc one rnd **below**, YO and pull up a loop, (YO and draw through 2 loops on hook) twice; repeat from ★ 2 times **more**, YO and draw through all 4 loops on hook.

PETAL (uses one sc)
YO 7 times, insert hook in sc indicated, YO and pull up a loop (9 loops on hook), (YO and draw through 2 loops on hook) 6 times, YO 6 times, insert hook in **same** st, YO and pull up a loop (10 loops on hook), (YO and draw through 2 loops on hook) 5 times, YO 5 times, insert hook in **same** st, YO and pull up a loop (11 loops on hook), (YO and draw through 2 loops on hook) 4 times, YO 4 times, insert hook in **same** st, YO and pull up a loop (12 loops on hook), (YO and draw through 2 loops on hook) 4 times (8 loops left on hook), YO and draw through 4 loops on hook (5 loops on hook), (YO and draw through 3 loops on hook) twice.

PICOT
Slip st in second ch from hook.

DECREASE (uses next 2 dc)
★ YO, insert hook in **next** dc, YO and pull up a loop, YO and draw through 2 loops on hook; repeat from ★ once **more**, place marker through 3 loops on hook for st placement, YO and draw through all 3 loops on hook **(counts as one dc)**.

DOUBLE DECREASE (uses next 3 dc)
★ YO, insert hook in **next** dc, YO and pull up a loop, YO and draw through 2 loops on hook; repeat from ★ 2 times **more**, place marker through last 3 loops on hook for st placement, YO and draw through all 4 loops on hook **(counts as one dc)**.

MOTIF A (Make 13)

With Green, ch 4; join with slip st to form a ring.

Rnd 1 (Right side)**:** Ch 1, 6 sc in ring; join with slip st to first sc, finish off.

Note: Loop a short piece of yarn around any stitch on Rnd 1 to mark **right** side.

Instructions continued on page 8.

Rnd 2: With **wrong** side facing and working in Back Loops Only ***(Fig. 2a, page 26)***, join Yellow with slip st in any sc; ch 2, (slip st in next sc, ch 2) around; join with slip st to **both** loops of joining slip st, finish off.

Rnd 3: With **right** side facing, working **behind** Rnd 2 in free loops of sc on Rnd 1 ***(Fig. 3a, page 26)***, join Green with sc in any sc ***(see Joining With Sc, page 26)***; ch 1, (sc in next sc, ch 1) 5 times; join with slip st to first sc, do **not** finish off.

Rnd 4: Working in Back Loops Only, slip st in next ch, ch 3 **(counts as first dc, now and throughout)**, 2 dc in same st, ch 2, skip next sc, ★ 3 dc in next ch, ch 2, skip next sc; repeat from ★ around; join with slip st to first dc: 18 dc and 6 ch-2 sps.

Rnd 5: Ch 3, working in both loops, dc in next 2 dc, ch 2, dc in next ch-2 sp, ch 2, ★ dc in next 3 dc, ch 2, dc in next ch-2 sp, ch 2; repeat from ★ around; join with slip st to first dc, finish off: 24 dc and 12 ch-2 sps.

Rnd 6: With **right** side facing, join Off-White with slip st in first ch-2 sp after joining; ch 4 **(counts as first tr)**, tr in same sp and in next dc, ch 2, 3 tr in next ch-2 sp, ch 2, skip next 3 dc, ★ 2 tr in next ch-2 sp, tr in next dc, ch 2, 3 tr in next ch-2 sp, ch 2, skip next 3 dc; repeat from ★ around; join with slip st to first tr, place loop from hook onto safety pin to keep piece from unraveling while you work the next rnd: 36 tr and 12 ch-2 sps.

Rnd 7: With **right** side facing and working Back Loops Only of tr and chs, skip next tr from joining and join Green with slip st in next tr; working slip sts **loosely**, slip st in next 6 sts, working in **front** of Rnd 6 and in skipped dc on Rnd 5, work Leaf, skip next ch on Rnd 6, ★ slip st in next 9 sts, working in **front** of Rnd 6 and in skipped dc on Rnd 5, work Leaf, skip next ch on Rnd 6; repeat from ★ around to last 2 tr, keeping loop and dropped yarn to **right** side, slip st in last 2 tr; join with slip st to **both** loops of joining slip st, finish off.

Rnd 8: Slip loop from safety pin onto hook, ch 1, working in **front** of Rnd 7 in free loops of sts on Rnd 6, sc in same st and in next 3 sts, ch 2, sc in next 4 sts, sc in **both** loops of next Leaf on Rnd 7, sc in next skipped ch on Rnd 6, ★ working in **front** of Rnd 7 in free loops of sts on Rnd 6, sc in next 4 sts, ch 2, sc in next 4 sts, sc in **both** loops of next Leaf on Rnd 7, sc in next skipped ch on Rnd 6; repeat from ★ around; join with slip st to first sc, place loop from hook onto safety pin to keep piece from unraveling while you work the next rnd: 60 sc and 6 ch-2 sps.

Rnd 9: With **right** side facing and working in Back Loops Only, join Red with slip st in first sc after joining; working slip sts **loosely**, slip st in next 2 sc, working in **front** of previous rnds, work Petal in Front Loop Only of skipped sc on Rnd 3 ***(Fig. 2a, page 26)***, skip next 2 chs on Rnd 8, ★ slip st in next 10 sc, working in **front** of previous rnds, work Petal in Front Loop Only of skipped sc on Rnd 3, skip next 2 chs on Rnd 8; repeat from ★ around to last 7 sc, keeping loop and dropped yarn to **right** side, slip st in last 7 sc; join with slip st to joining slip st, finish off: 6 Petals made.

Rnd 10: Slip loop from safety pin onto hook, ch 1, working in **front** of Rnd 9 in free loops of sc on Rnd 8, sc in first 3 sc, hdc in next sc, (hdc, dc) in Front Loop Only of next ch ***(Fig. 2b, page 26)***, skip next Petal and next ch, 2 hdc in next sc, ★ sc in next 8 sc, hdc in next sc, (hdc, dc) in Front Loop Only of next ch, skip next Petal and next ch, 2 hdc in next sc; repeat from ★ around to last 5 sc, sc in last 5 sc; join with slip st to first sc.

Rnd 11: Working in **both** loops of sts on Rnd 10 **and** in Back Loops Only of sts on Rnd 9 (both rnds together), ★ slip st in next st, ch 4, skip next 2 sts, slip st in next st, ch 6, place marker around ch-6 to mark corner, skip next 2 sts, slip st in next st, ch 4, skip next 2 sts, slip st in next st, ch 5, skip next 3 sts; repeat from ★ around; join with slip st to first slip st, finish off: 24 sps.

MOTIF B (Make 20)

With Off-White, ch 4; join with slip st to form a ring.

Rnd 1: Ch 5, work Picot **(3 skipped chs count as first dc)**, ch 1, ★ dc in ring, ch 2, work Picot, ch 1; repeat from ★ 4 times **more**; join with slip st to first dc: 6 dc and 6 Picots.

Rnd 2 (Right side)**:** Ch 3, turn; 2 dc in same st, ch 3, skip next Picot, ★ 3 dc in next dc, ch 3, skip next Picot; repeat from ★ around; join with slip st to first dc: 18 dc and 6 ch-3 sps.

Note: Mark Rnd 2 as **right** side.

Rnd 3: Ch 3, do **not** turn; dc in next 2 dc, ch 5, slip st in next ch-3 sp, ch 5, ★ dc in next 3 dc, ch 5, slip st in next ch-3 sp, ch 5; repeat from ★ around; join with slip st to first dc: 18 dc and 12 ch-5 sps.

Rnd 4: Ch 2, decrease, ch 5, slip st in next 2 ch-5 sps, ch 5, ★ work double decrease, ch 5, slip st in next 2 ch-5 sps, ch 5; repeat from ★ around; join with slip st to first dc.

Rnd 5: Slip st in next 2 chs and in same sp, ch 6, skip next slip st, slip st in next slip st, ch 6, slip st in next ch-5 sp, ch 4, tr in 3 marked loops of next dc ***(Fig. A)***, ch 4, ★ slip st in next ch-5 sp, ch 6, skip next slip st, slip st in next slip st, ch 6, slip st in next ch-5 sp, ch 4, tr in 3 marked loops of next dc; ch 4; repeat from ★ around; skip first 2 slip sts and join with slip st to next slip st: 24 sps.

Fig. A

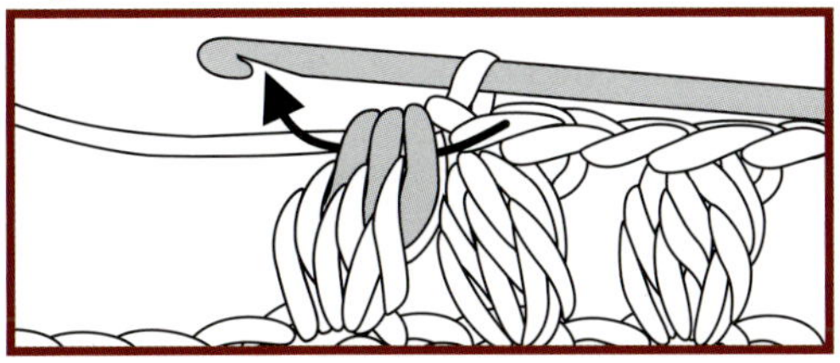

Rnd 6: Slip st in next 2 chs and in same sp, ch 2, tr in next slip st, ch 2, slip st in next ch-6 sp, ch 5, slip st in next ch-4 sp, ch 6, place marker around ch-6 to mark corner, slip st in next ch-4 sp, ch 5, ★ slip st in next ch-6 sp, ch 2, tr in next slip st, ch 2, slip st in next ch-6 sp, ch 5, slip st in next ch-4 sp, ch 6, place marker around ch-6 to mark corner, slip st in next ch-4 sp, ch 5; repeat from ★ around; skip first 2 slip sts and join with slip st to next slip st, finish off.

ASSEMBLY

Using Diagram as a guide for placement and beginning with first Motif, join Motifs as follows:

Placement Diagram

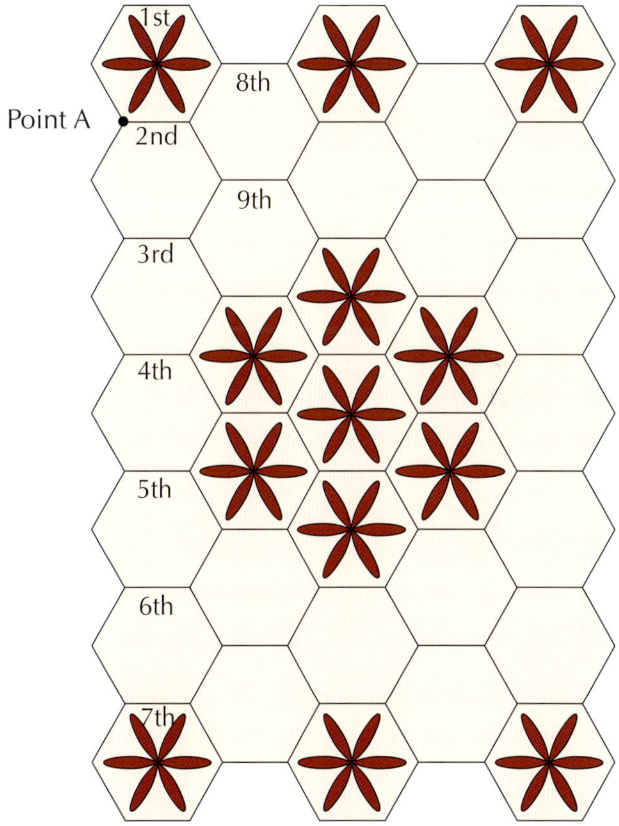

Instructions continued on page 10.

To make an afghan that can be used all year long choose different colors as shown above.

FIRST MOTIF A EDGING

With **right** side of Motif A facing, join Yellow with slip st in first ch-4 sp after any marked ch-6 sp; ch 5, slip st in next ch-5 sp, ch 3, slip st in next ch-4 sp, ch 5, slip st in next corner ch-6 sp, ch 5, ★ slip st in next ch-4 sp, ch 3, slip st in next ch-5 sp, ch 3, slip st in next ch-4 sp, ch 5, slip st in next corner ch-6 sp, ch 5; repeat from ★ around; join with slip st to joining slip st, finish off.

SECOND MOTIF

With **right** side of Motif B facing, join Yellow with slip st in first ch-5 sp after any marked ch-6 sp; ch 3, skip next ch-2 sp, slip st in next tr, ch 3, skip next ch-2 sp, slip st in next ch-5 sp, ch 5, slip st in next corner ch-6 sp, ★ ch 5, slip st in next ch-5 sp, ch 3, skip next ch-2 sp, slip st in next tr, ch 3, skip next ch-2 sp, slip st in next ch-5 sp, ch 5, slip st in next corner ch-6 sp; repeat from ★ 3 times **more**, ch 2, holding Motif A and Motif B with **wrong** sides together, slip st in corresponding ch-5 sp on **First Motif**, ch 2, slip st in next ch-5 sp on **Second Motif**, ch 1, slip st in next ch-3 sp on **First Motif**, ch 1, skip next ch-2 sp on **Second Motif**, slip st in next tr, ch 1, slip st in next ch-3 sp on **First Motif**, ch 1, skip next ch-2 sp on **Second Motif**, slip st in next ch-5 sp, ch 2, slip st in next ch-5 sp on **First Motif**, ch 2, slip st in last corner ch-6 sp on **Second Motif**, ch 5; join with slip st to joining slip st, finish off.

THIRD THROUGH SIXTH MOTIFS

With **right** side of next Motif B facing, join Yellow with slip st in first ch-5 sp after any corner ch-6 sp; ch 3, skip next ch-2 sp, slip st in next tr, ch 3, skip next ch-2 sp, slip st in next ch-5 sp, ch 5, slip st in next corner ch-6 sp, ★ ch 5, slip st in next ch-5 sp, ch 3, skip next ch-2 sp, slip st in next tr, ch 3, skip next ch-2 sp, slip st in next ch-5 sp, ch 5, slip st in next corner ch-6 sp; repeat from ★ 3 times **more**, ch 2, holding Motifs with **wrong** sides together, slip st in corresponding ch-5 sp on **previous Motif**, ch 2, slip st in next ch-5 sp on **new Motif**, ch 1, slip st in next ch-3 sp on **previous Motif**, ch 1, skip next ch-2 sp on **new Motif**, slip st in next tr, ch 1, slip st in next ch-3 sp on **previous Motif**, ch 1, skip next ch-2 sp on **new Motif**, slip st in next ch-5 sp, ch 2, slip st in next ch-5 sp on **previous Motif**, ch 2, slip st in last corner ch-6 sp on **new Motif**, ch 5; join with slip st to joining slip st, finish off.

SEVENTH MOTIF

With **right** side of next Motif A facing, join Yellow with slip st in first ch-4 sp after any marked ch-6 sp; ch 3, slip st in next ch-5 sp, ch 3, slip st in next ch-4 sp, ch 5, slip st in next corner ch-6 sp, ★ ch 5, slip st in next ch-4 sp, ch 3, slip st in next ch-5 sp, ch 3, slip st in next ch-4 sp, ch 5, slip st in next corner ch-6 sp; repeat from ★ 3 times **more**, ch 2, holding Motif A and Motif B with **wrong** sides together, slip st in corresponding ch-5 sp on **previous Motif**, ch 2, slip st in next ch-4 sp on **new Motif**, ch 1, slip st in next ch-3 sp on **previous Motif**, ch 1, slip st in next ch-5 sp on **new Motif**, ch 1, slip st in next ch-3 sp on **previous Motif**, ch 1, slip st in next ch-4 sp on **new Motif**, ch 2, slip st in next ch-5 sp on **previous Motif**, ch 2, slip st in last corner ch-6 sp on **new Motif**, ch 5; join with slip st to joining slip st, finish off.

EIGHTH MOTIF (Two Side Joining)

With **right** side of next Motif B facing, join Yellow with slip st in first ch-5 sp after any corner ch-6 sp; ch 3, skip next ch-2 sp, slip st in next tr, ch 3, skip next ch-2 sp, slip st in next ch-5 sp, ch 5, slip st in next corner ch-6 sp, ★ ch 5, slip st in next ch-5 sp, ch 3, skip next ch-2 sp, slip st in next tr, ch 3, skip next ch-2 sp, slip st in next ch-5 sp, ch 5, slip st in next corner ch-6 sp; repeat from ★ 2 times **more**, † ch 2, holding Motifs with **wrong** sides together, slip st in corresponding ch-5 sp on **adjacent Motif**, ch 2, slip st in next ch-5 sp on **new Motif**, ch 1, slip st in next ch-3 sp on **adjacent Motif**, ch 1, skip next ch-2 sp on **new Motif**, slip st in next tr, ch 1, slip st in next ch-3 sp on **adjacent Motif**, ch 1, skip next ch-2 sp on **new Motif**, slip st in next ch-5 sp, ch 2, slip st in next ch-5 sp on **adjacent Motif**, ch 2, slip st in next corner ch-6 sp on **new Motif** †; repeat from † to † once **more**, ch 5; join with slip st to joining slip st, finish off.

NINTH MOTIF (Three Side Joining)

With **right** side of next Motif B facing, join Yellow with slip st in first ch-5 sp after any corner ch-6 sp; ch 3, skip next ch-2 sp, slip st in next tr, ch 3, skip next ch-2 sp, slip st in next ch-5 sp, ch 5, slip st in next corner ch-6 sp, ★ ch 5, slip st in next ch-5 sp, ch 3, skip next ch-2 sp, slip st in next tr, ch 3, skip next ch-2 sp, slip st in next ch-5 sp, ch 5, slip st in next corner ch-6 sp; repeat from ★ once **more**, † ch 2, holding Motifs with **wrong** sides together, slip st in corresponding ch-5 sp on **adjacent Motif**, ch 2, slip st in next ch-5 sp on **new Motif**, ch 1, slip st in next ch-3 sp on **adjacent Motif**, ch 1, skip next ch-2 sp on **new Motif**, slip st in next tr, ch 1, slip st in next ch-3 sp on **adjacent Motif**, ch 1, skip next ch-2 sp on **new Motif**, slip st in next ch-5 sp, ch 2, slip st in next ch-5 sp on **adjacent Motif**, ch 2, slip st in next corner ch-6 sp on **new Motif** †; repeat from † to † 2 times **more**, ch 5; join with slip st to joining slip st, finish off.

REMAINING MOTIFS

Join remaining Motifs in same manner when joining to Motif A, working in ch-3 sps and when joining to Motif B, working in tr.

EDGING

Rnd 1: With **right** side facing, join Yellow with slip st to Second Motif in first free ch-sp after joining (point A); ch 1, slip st in same sp, † ★ [ch 4, (slip st, ch 1, slip st) in next sp] 3 times, ch 6, (slip st, ch 1, slip st) in next sp, [ch 4, (slip st, ch 1, slip st) in next sp] 3 times, ch 3, skip next joining, (slip st, ch 1, slip st) in first free ch-sp on next Motif; repeat from ★ 4 times **more**, ♥ [ch 4, (slip st, ch 1, slip st) in next sp] 3 times, ch 6, (slip st, ch 1, slip st) in next sp ♥; repeat from ♥ to ♥ twice, [ch 4, (slip st, ch 1, slip st) in next sp] 3 times, ch 3, skip next joining, (slip st, ch 1, slip st) in first free ch-sp on next Motif, [ch 4, (slip st, ch 1, slip st) in next sp] 3 times, ch 3, skip next joining, (slip st, ch 1, slip st) in first free ch-sp on next Motif, repeat from ♥ to ♥ twice, [ch 4, (slip st, ch 1, slip st) in next sp] 3 times, ch 3, skip next joining, (slip st, ch 1, slip st) in first free ch-sp on next Motif, [ch 4, (slip st, ch 1, slip st) in next sp] 3 times, ch 3, skip next joining, (slip st, ch 1, slip st) in first free ch-sp on next Motif, repeat from ♥ to ♥ 3 times, [ch 4, (slip st, ch 1, slip st) in next sp] 3 times, ch 3, skip next joining †, (slip st, ch 1, slip st) in first free ch-sp on next Motif; repeat from † to † once **more**; join with slip st to joining slip st.

Rnd 2: Slip st in next ch-1 sp, skip next slip st, , ★ † ♥ [(slip st, ch 3) twice in next ch-4 sp] 3 times, (slip st, ch 3) 4 times in next ch-6 sp ♥, [(slip st, ch 3) twice in next ch-4 sp] 2 times, (slip st, ch 3, slip st) in next ch-4 sp, ch 2, slip st in ch-3 sp, ch 2 †; repeat from † to † 3 times **more**, repeat from ♥ to ♥ 3 times, [(slip st, ch 3) twice in next ch-4 sp] 2 times, (slip st, ch 3, slip st) in next ch-4 sp, ch 2, slip st in ch-3 sp, ch 2, [(slip st, ch 3) twice in next ch-4 sp] 2 times, (slip st, ch 3, slip st) in next ch-4 sp, ch 2, slip st in ch-3 sp, ch 2, repeat from ♥ to ♥ twice, [(slip st, ch 3) twice in next ch-4 sp] 2 times, (slip st, ch 3, slip st) in next ch-4 sp, ch 2, slip st in ch-3 sp, ch 2, [(slip st, ch 3) twice in next ch-4 sp] across to next ch-3 sp, ch 2, slip st in ch-3 sp, ch 2, repeat from ♥ to ♥ 3 times, [(slip st, ch 3) twice in next ch-4 sp] 2 times, (slip st, ch 3, slip st) in next ch-4 sp, ch 2; repeat from ★ once **more**, skip first 2 slip sts and join with slip st to next slip st, finish off.

Spice GARDENS

INTERMEDIATE

Finished Size: 50" x 69" (127 cm x 175 cm)

MATERIALS

Medium Weight Yarn MEDIUM 4
[3.5 ounces, 170 yards
(100 grams, 156 meters) per skein]:
Off-White - 5 skeins
Orange - 4 skeins
Rust - 3 skeins
Yellow - 2 skeins
Crochet hook, size J (6 mm) **or** size needed for gauge

GAUGE SWATCH: 3" (7.5 cm)
Work 4 Petals; slip st in same ch as First Petal, finish off: one Flower.

STITCH GUIDE

TREBLE CROCHET *(abbreviated tr)*
YO twice, insert hook in st indicated, YO and pull up a loop (4 loops on hook), (YO and draw through 2 loops on hook) 3 times.

PETAL
Ch 6, (3 tr, ch 5, slip st) in sixth ch from hook.

FIRST HALF PETAL
Ch 6, 2 tr in sixth ch from hook.

SECOND HALF PETAL
(Tr, ch 5, slip st) in free loops of same ch as next Half Petal ***(Fig. 3b, page 26)***.

Instructions continued on page 14.

FLOWER STRIP

CENTER (Make 6 with Orange, 4 with Red, and 3 with Yellow)

Work Petal twice, work First Half Petal twice, (work Petal, work First Half Petal twice) 20 times, work Petal 3 times; working across opposite side of Center, slip st in same ch as third Petal from hook, work Second Half Petal twice, ★ work Petal, slip st in same ch as Petal on opposite side, work Second Half Petal twice; repeat from ★ across to last 2 Petals, work Petal; slip st in same ch as first Petal, finish off: 22 4-Petal Flowers.

Note: Loop a short piece of yarn around any stitch on second Petal made to mark **right** side and bottom edge of Center.

EDGING AND JOINING

Use Diagram as a guide for placement. Strips are joined starting with First Flower Strip on the left and working to the right on Afghan.

Placement Diagram

FIRST FLOWER STRIP

Rnd 1: With **right** side facing, having bottom edge to the right, and working in Back Loop **and** horizontal bar of tr ***(Fig. A)*** **or** in top two loops of chs ***(Fig. B)***, join Ecru with slip st in fifth ch before first tr on marked Petal; ch 4, † skip next 2 tr, slip st in next tr, ch 4, slip st in third ch on next Petal, ch 5, slip st in third ch on next Petal, ch 4, slip st in fifth ch on next Petal, ch 4 †; repeat from † to † across to last Flower, skip next 2 tr, slip st in next tr, ch 3, slip st in fifth ch on next Petal, ch 3, skip next tr, slip st in next tr, ch 3, skip next tr, slip st in next ch, ch 3, slip st in fifth ch on next Petal, ch 4, ★ skip next 2 tr, slip st in next tr, ch 4, slip st in second ch on next Petal, ch 5, slip st in second ch on next Petal, ch 4, slip st in fifth ch on next Petal, ch 4; repeat from ★ across to last Flower, skip next 2 tr, slip st in next tr, ch 3, slip st in fifth ch on next Petal, ch 3, skip next tr, slip st in next tr, ch 3, skip next tr, slip st in next ch, ch 3; join with slip st to joining slip st.

Fig. A

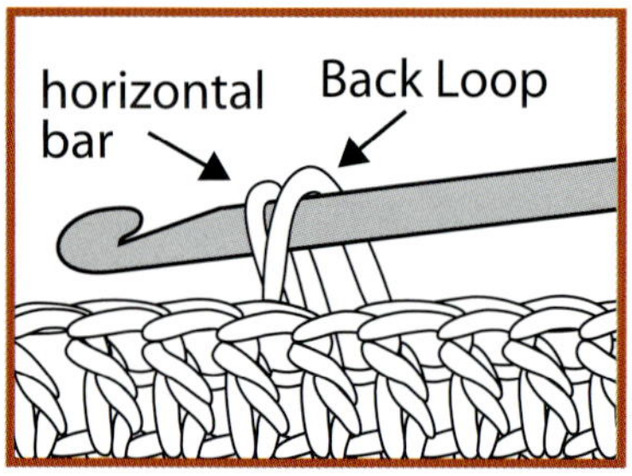

Fig. B

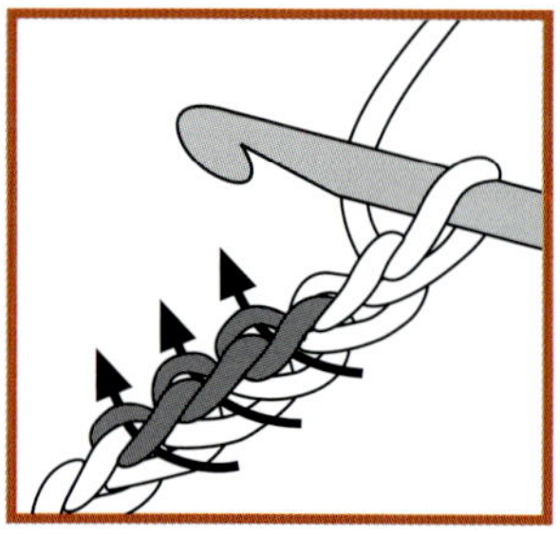

Rnd 2: (Slip st, ch 3, slip st) in first ch-4 sp, † ★ ch 5, skip next ch-4 sp, slip st in next ch-5 sp, ch 5, skip next ch-4 sp, (slip st, ch 3, slip st) in next ch-4 sp; repeat from ★ across to last Flower, ch 5, (slip st in next ch-3 sp, ch 5) 4 times †, (slip st, ch 3, slip st) in next ch-4 sp, place marker around ch-3 just made for placement, repeat from † to † once **more**; join with slip st to joining slip st, finish off.

STRIP JOINING

Work same as First Flower Strip through Rnd 1.

Rnd 2: (Slip st, ch 3, slip st) in first ch-4 sp, ★ ch 5, skip next ch-4 sp, slip st in next ch-5 sp, ch 5, skip next ch-4 sp, (slip st, ch 3, slip st) in next ch-4 sp; repeat from ★ across to last Flower, (ch 5, slip st in next ch-3 sp) 4 times, ch 2, holding two Strips with **wrong** sides together and markers at same end, slip st in corresponding ch-5 sp on **previous Strip**, ch 2, slip st in next ch-4 sp on **new Strip**, ch 1, slip st in next ch-3 sp on **previous Strip**, ch 1, slip st in same ch-4 sp on **new Strip**, † ch 1, slip st in next ch-5 sp on **previous Strip**, ch 3, skip next ch-4 sp on **new Strip**, slip st in next ch-5 sp, ch 3, slip st in next ch-5 sp on **previous Strip**, ch 1, skip next ch-4 sp on **new Strip**, slip st in next ch-4 sp, ch 1, slip st in next ch-3 sp on **previous Strip**, ch 1, slip st in same ch-4 sp on **new Strip** †; repeat from † to † across to last 4 ch-3 sps on **new Strip**, ch 1, slip st in next ch-5 sp on **previous Strip**, ch 2, slip st in next ch-3 sp on **new Strip**, ch 5, (slip st in next ch-3 sp, ch 5) 3 times; join with slip st to joining slip st, finish off.

Join remaining Flower Strips in same manner; at end of last Flower Strip; do **not** finish off, slip st in next ch-3 sp.

EDGING

FIRST SIDE

Row 1: Ch 5, turn; (slip st in next ch-5 sp, ch 5) 4 times, slip st around next joining, ★ ch 5, (slip st in next ch-5 sp, ch 5) 3 times, slip st around joining; repeat from ★ across to last Strip, (ch 5, slip st in next ch-5 sp) 5 times; finish off.

Row 2: With **right** side facing, join Ecru with slip st in second ch-5 sp on Row 1; (ch 5, slip st) twice in each of next 2 ch-5 sps, ★ ch 3, slip st in next ch-5 sp, ch 2, slip st in next ch-5 sp, ch 3, (slip st, ch 5) twice in next ch-5 sp, (slip st, ch 5, slip st) in next ch-5 sp; repeat from ★ across to last 2 ch-5 sps, ch 5, slip st in next ch-5 sp, leave last ch-5 sp unworked; finish off.

SECOND SIDE

Row 1: With **wrong** side facing, join Ecru with slip st in marked ch-3 sp on First Flower Strip; ch 5, (slip st in next ch-5 sp, ch 5) 4 times, slip st around next joining, ★ ch 5, (slip st in next ch-5 sp, ch 5) 3 times, slip st around joining; repeat from ★ across to last Strip, (ch 5, slip st in next ch-5 sp) 5 times; finish off.

Row 2: Work same as First Side.

Garden TRELLIS

INTERMEDIATE

Finished Size: 49" x 66" (124.5 cm x 167.5 cm)

MATERIALS

BULKY 5

Bulky Weight Yarn
[2.80 ounces, 128 yards
(80 grams, 117 meters) per skein]:
Ecru - 7 skeins
Blue - 6 skeins
Crochet hook, size K (6.5 mm) **or** size needed for gauge

GAUGE: 8 dc and 4 rows = 3" (7.5 cm)
Solid Panel - $8^{1}/_{4}$" (21 cm) wide
Flower Panel - 12" (30.5 cm) wide

Gauge Swatch: $8^{1}/_{4}$" x 3" (21 cm x 7.5 cm)
Work same as Solid Panel, page 19; do **not** finish off.

STITCH GUIDE

LOWER PETAL

YO 3 times, insert hook in st indicated, YO and pull up a loop, (YO and draw through 2 loops on hook) 3 times, YO twice, insert hook in wrap **and** in one front leg of last st made ***(Fig. 4, page 27)***, YO and pull up a loop, (YO and draw through 2 loops on hook) twice, YO twice, insert hook in same st, YO and pull up a loop, (YO and draw through 2 loops on hook) twice.

TOP PETAL

★ YO twice, insert hook in st indicated, YO and pull up a loop, (YO and draw through 2 loops on hook) twice; repeat from ★ 2 times **more**, YO and draw through 3 loops on hook, YO and draw through 2 loops on hook.

2-TR CLUSTER (uses one st)

★ YO twice, insert hook in st indicated, YO and pull up a loop, (YO and draw through 2 loops on hook) twice; repeat from ★ once **more**, YO and draw through all 3 loops on hook **(counts as one tr)**.

Instructions continued on page 18.

FLOWER PANEL (Make 2)

With Blue, ch 51; place marker in first and in last ch for joining placement.

Row 1 (Right side)**:** ★ ♥ † YO twice, insert hook in back ridge of third ch from hook ***(Fig. 1, page 26)***, YO and pull up a loop, (YO and draw through 2 loops on hook) twice †; repeat from † to † once **more** (3 loops on hook), skip next 4 chs, work Lower Petal in next ch (6 loops on hook), skip next 5 chs, work Lower Petal in next ch (9 loops on hook), YO and draw through all 9 loops on hook, ch 1 to close **(Flower Center made)**, ch 3, work 2-tr Cluster in Flower Center, ch 1, skip next 4 chs, sc in next ch ♥, ch 3; repeat from ★ once **more**, then repeat from ♥ to ♥ once: 3 4-Petal groups.

Note: Loop a short piece of yarn around any stitch to mark Row 1 as **right** side and bottom edge.

Row 2: Ch 1, turn; sc in first sc, ★ † ch 4, work (Top Petal, ch 9, Top Petal) in next Flower Center, ch 4 †, sc in next sc; repeat from ★ once **more**, then repeat from † to † once, sc in free loop of ch at base of Last Petal ***(Fig. 3b, page 26)***: 3 6-Petal Flowers.

Row 3: Ch 4, turn; work Lower Petal in next Top Petal, YO and draw through all 4 loops on hook, ch 4, work 2-tr Cluster in back ridge of fourth ch from hook, ★ † ch 1, skip next 4 chs, sc in next ch, ch 3, ♥ YO twice, insert hook in back ridge of third ch from hook, YO and pull up a loop, (YO and draw through 2 loops on hook) twice ♥; repeat from ♥ to ♥ once **more** (3 loops on hook), work Lower Petal in next Top Petal †, skip next sc, work Lower Petal in next Top Petal, YO and draw through all 9 loops on hook, ch 1 **(Flower Center made)**, ch 3, work 2-tr Cluster in Flower Center; repeat from ★ once **more**, repeat from † to † once, YO 3 times, insert hook in last sc, YO and pull up a loop, (YO and draw through 2 loops on hook) 3 times (7 loops on hook), YO and draw through all 7 loops on hook.

Row 4: Ch 10, turn; work Top Petal in first partial Flower Center, ch 4, sc in next sc, ch 4, ★ work (Top Petal, ch 9, Top Petal) in next Flower Center, ch 4, sc in next sc, ch 4; repeat from ★ once **more**, work Top Petal in top of last Lower Petal.

Row 5: Ch 8, turn; † YO twice, insert hook in back ridge of third ch from hook, YO and pull up a loop, (YO and draw through 2 loops on hook) twice †; repeat from † to † once **more** (3 loops on hook), ★ ♥ work Lower Petal in top of next Top Petal, skip next sc, work Lower Petal in top of next Top Petal, YO and draw through all 9 loops on hook, ch 1 **(Flower Center made)**, ch 3, work 2-tr Cluster in Flower Center, ch 1 ♥, skip next 4 chs, sc in next ch, ch 3, repeat from † to † twice (3 loops on hook); repeat from ★ once **more**; then repeat from ♥ to ♥ once, skip next 4 chs, sc in next ch.

Rows 6-43: Repeat Rows 2-5, 9 times; then repeat Rows 2 and 3 once **more**: 21 rows of Flowers and one row of partial Flowers.

Row 44: Ch 3, † YO twice, insert hook in first partial Flower Center, YO and pull up a loop, (YO and draw through 2 loops on hook) twice †; repeat from † to † once **more** (3 loops on hook), (YO and draw through 2 loops on hook) twice, ch 3, sc in next sc, ch 3, ★ work (Top Petal, ch 3, Top Petal) in next Flower Center, ch 3, sc in next sc, ch 3; repeat from ★ once **more**, work Top Petal in top of last Lower Petal; finish off.

EMBELLISHMENT ACCENTS

Notes: Embellishment Accents are worked in spaces diagonally across Flower Panel. As you work the first few lines, they may look bunched up, but they will straighten out and stretch as more lines are added.

With Ecru, make a slip knot on hook. With **right** side of Panel facing and keeping yarn on **wrong** side throughout, slip st in any ch-4 sp on Row 1; ch 1, (slip st, ch 1) 4 times in each sp across to edge, slip st around edge st; finish off.

Repeat for remaining Embellishment Accents.

SOLID PANEL (Make 3)

With Ecru, ch 24.

Row 1: Dc in fourth ch from hook **(3 skipped chs count as first dc)** and next 2 chs, † ch 1, skip next ch, dc in next ch, place marker around dc just made for st placement, dc in next 3 chs, place marker around last dc made for st placement, ch 1, skip next ch †, dc in next 2 chs, repeat from † to † once, dc in last 4 chs: 18 dc and 4 ch-1 sps.

Note: Mark on Row 1 as **right** side and bottom edge.

Row 2: Ch 3 **(counts as first dc, now and throughout)**, turn; dc in next 3 dc, ch 1, dc in next 4 dc, ch 1, dc in next 2 dc, (ch 1, dc in next 4 dc) twice.

Repeat Row 2 until Panel measures same as completed Flower Panel, ending by working a **right** side row; finish off.

Place markers around dc on last row in same manner as on Row 1.

EMBELLISHMENT

Column 1: Beginning on last row of Panel and ending at Row 1, join Blue with slip st around first marked dc on last row; ★ ch 6, skip dc on next row, slip st around dc on next row; repeat from ★ across; finish off.

Column 2: Beginning on Row 1 of Panel and ending at last row, join Blue with slip st around second marked dc on Row 1; ★ ch 3, slip st in corresponding ch-6 sp of previous Column, ch 2, skip dc on next row, slip st around dc on next row; repeat from ★ across; finish off.

Columns 3 and 4: Repeat Columns 1 and 2 beginning at remaining two marked dc.

ASSEMBLY

Alternate Panels as follows: Solid Panel, (Flower Panel, Solid Panel) twice.
When joining Panels, work around each dc along edge of Solid Panel **and** around sps, sts, and in Flower Centers along edge of Flower Panel.
Hold Panels with **wrong** sides together, Flower Panel facing, matching bottom of Solid Panel with marked end of beginning ch of Flower Panel.
Join Ecru with slip st at top edge, working from **left** to **right**, [ch 1, work reverse sc **loosely** ***(Figs. 5a-d, page 27)***] evenly across; finish off.

Holding four 12" (30.5 cm) strands of Blue together, add fringe evenly spaced across each short edge of Afghan ***(Figs. 6a & b, page 27)***.

Town SQUARE

INTERMEDIATE

Finished Size: 49½" x 68" (125.5 cm x 172.5 cm)

MATERIALS

Medium Weight Yarn (MEDIUM 4)
[3 ounces, 197 yards
(85 grams, 180 meters) per skein]:
Ecru - 12 skeins
Purple - 3 skeins
Green - 1 skein
Rust - 1 skein
Crochet hook, size J (6 mm) **or** size needed for gauge
Safety pin

GAUGE: Each Square = 9½" (24 cm)

Gauge Swatch: 5" (12.75 cm) square
Work same as 3-Color Square through Rnd 4, page 22.

STITCH GUIDE

TREBLE CROCHET ***(abbreviated tr)***
YO twice, insert hook in st indicated, YO and pull up a loop (4 loops on hook), (YO and draw through 2 loops on hook) 3 times.

BEGINNING CLUSTER (uses one ch)
★ YO twice, insert hook in ch indicated, YO and pull up a loop, (YO and draw through 2 loops on hook) twice; repeat from ★ once **more**, YO and draw through all 3 loops on hook.

CLUSTER (uses one ch)
★ YO twice, insert hook in ch indicated, YO and pull up a loop, (YO and draw through 2 loops on hook) twice; repeat from ★ 2 times **more**, YO and draw through all 4 loops on hook.

Instructions continued on page 22.

3-COLOR SQUARE (Make 23)

With Purple, ch 8; being careful not to twist ch, join with slip st to form a ring.

Rnd 1 (Wrong side)**:** Working in back ridge of chs ***(Fig. 1, page 26)***, (slip st, ch 4, work beginning Cluster) in next ch, ch 6, ★ skip next ch, work Cluster in next ch, ch 6; repeat from ★ 2 times **more**; skip next slip st and beginning Cluster and join with slip st in **both** loops of next ch, finish off: 4 Clusters.

Note: Loop a short piece of yarn around **back** of any stitch on Rnd 1 to mark **right** side.

Rnd 2: With **right** side facing, join Ecru with sc in any ch-6 sp ***(see Joining With Sc, page 26)***; ★ † working in **front** of same ch-6, tr in Front Loop Only of next skipped ch on beginning ch ***(Fig. 2b, page 26)***, sc in same ch-6 sp, working in **front** of same ch-6, dc in wrap **and** in one front leg of last tr made ***(Fig. 4, page 27)***, sc in same ch-6 sp, (2 sc, ch 1, 2 sc) in next Cluster †, sc in next ch-6 sp; repeat from ★ 2 times **more**, then repeat from † to † once; join with slip st to Back Loop Only of first sc ***(Fig. 2a, page 26)***.

Rnd 3: Ch 3 **(counts as first dc, now and throughout)**, working in Back Loops Only, dc in next 6 sts, (dc, ch 3, dc) in next ch, ★ dc in next 9 sts, (dc, ch 3, dc) in next ch; repeat from ★ 2 times **more**, dc in last 2 sc; join with slip st to first dc: 44 dc and 12 chs.

Rnd 4: Ch 3, working in Back Loops Only, ★ dc in next 8 sts, (dc, ch 5, dc) in next ch, ★ dc in next 13 sts, (dc, ch 5, dc) in next ch; repeat from ★ 2 times **more**, dc in next ch and in last 3 dc; join with slip st to first dc, slip loop from hook onto safety pin to keep piece from unraveling while working Rnd 5: 60 dc and 20 chs.

Rnd 5: With **right** side facing and keeping loop **behind** sts being worked, join Green with slip st in Back Loop Only of center ch of first corner ch-5 after joining; slip st in Back Loop Only of next 3 sts, working in **front** of Rnd 4, tr in free loop of center ch one rnd **below** ***(Fig. 3c, page 26)***, skip next dc on Rnd 4, slip st in Front Loop Only of next 12 dc, ★ working in **front** of Rnd 4, tr in free loop of center ch one rnd **below**, skip next dc on Rnd 4, slip st in Back Loop Only of next 6 sts, working in **front** of Rnd 4, tr in same ch one rnd **below** as last tr made, skip next dc on Rnd 4, slip st in Front Loop Only of next 12 dc; repeat from ★ 2 times **more**, working in **front** of Rnd 4, tr in free loop of same ch one rnd **below** as first tr made, skip next dc on Rnd 4, slip st in Back Loop Only of last 2 chs; join with slip st to **both** loops of joining slip st, finish off: 80 sts.

Rnd 6: Place loop from safety pin onto hook, working **behind** Rnd 5, ch 3, dc in free loop of next 9 dc, dc in Back Loop Only of next skipped dc, dc in next 2 chs, (dc, ch 5, dc) in next ch, dc in next 2 chs and in next dc, dc in Back Loop Only of next skipped dc, ★ dc in free loop of next 12 dc, dc in Back Loop Only of next skipped dc, dc in next 2 chs, (dc, ch 5, dc) in next ch, dc in next 2 chs and in next dc, dc in Back Loop Only of next skipped dc; repeat from ★ 2 times **more**, dc in free loop of last 2 dc; join with slip st to first dc, slip loop from hook onto safety pin to keep piece from unraveling while working Rnd 7: 84 dc and 20 chs.

Rnd 7: With **right** side facing and keeping loop **behind** sts being worked, join Rust with slip st in Back Loop Only of center ch of first corner ch-5 after joining; slip st in Back Loop Only of next 3 sts, working in **front** of Rnd 6, tr in free loop of center ch one rnd **below**, skip next dc on Rnd 6, slip st in Front Loop Only of next 18 dc, ★ working in **front** of Rnd 6, tr in free loop of center ch one rnd **below**, skip next dc on Rnd 6, slip st in Back Loop Only of next 6 sts, working in **front** of Rnd 6, tr in same ch one rnd **below** as last tr made, skip next dc on Rnd 6, slip st in Front Loop Only of next 18 dc; repeat from ★ 2 times **more**, working in **front** of Rnd 6, tr in free loop of same ch one rnd **below** as first tr made, skip next dc on Rnd 6, slip st in Back Loop Only of last 2 chs; join with slip st to **both** loops of joining slip st, finish off: 104 sts.

Rnd 8: Place loop from safety pin onto hook, working **behind** Rnd 7, ch 3, dc in free loop of next 12 dc, dc in Back Loop Only of next skipped dc, dc in next 2 chs, (dc, ch 5, dc) in next ch, dc in next 2 chs and in next dc, dc in Back Loop Only of next skipped dc, ★ dc in free loop of next 18 dc, dc in Back Loop Only of next skipped dc, dc in next 2 chs, (dc, ch 5, dc) in next ch, dc in next 2 chs and in next dc, dc in Back Loop Only of next skipped dc; repeat from ★ 2 times **more**, dc in free loop of last 5 dc; join with slip st to first dc, finish off: 108 dc and 20 chs.

Rnd 9: With **right** side facing, join Purple with slip st in Back Loop Only of center ch of first corner ch-5 after joining; slip st in Back Loop Only of next 3 sts, working in **front** of Rnd 8, tr in free loop of center ch one rnd **below**, skip next dc on Rnd 8, slip st in Front Loop Only of next 24 dc, ★ working in **front** of Rnd 8, tr in free loop of center ch one rnd **below**, skip next dc on Rnd 8, slip st in Back Loop Only of next 6 sts, working in **front** of Rnd 8, tr in same ch one rnd **below** as last tr made, skip next dc on Rnd 8, slip st in Front Loop Only of next 24 dc; repeat from ★ 2 times **more**, working in **front** of Rnd 8, tr in free loop of same ch one rnd **below** as first tr made, skip next dc on Rnd 8, slip st in Back Loop Only of last 2 chs; join with slip st to **both** loops of joining slip st, finish off: 128 sts.

Rnd 10: With **right** side facing and working **behind** Rnd 9 in free loop of sts on Rnd 8 and in Back Loops Only of skipped dc, join Ecru with dc in center ch of any corner ch-5 ***(see Joining With Dc, page 26)***; ch 3, dc in same st, ch 1, (skip next st, dc in next st, ch 1) 15 times, skip next ch, ★ (dc, ch 3, dc) in next center ch, ch 1, (skip next st, dc in next st, ch 1) 15 times, skip next ch; repeat from ★ 2 times **more**; join with slip st to first dc, finish off: 17 dc and 16 ch-1 sps **each** side (68 dc and 68 sps total).

SOLID COLOR SQUARE

(Make 12)

Using Ecru for entire Square, work same as 3-Color Square, page 22.

Instructions continued on page 24.

ASSEMBLY

Using Diagram as a guide for placement, join Squares into 5 vertical strips of 7 Squares each.

Join two Squares as follows:
With **right** side of two Squares facing, slightly overlap side edges.
With Purple, make a slip knot on hook. Working through Back Loops Only of sts on **both** pieces and holding yarn to **wrong** side of pieces; slip st in center ch of first corner; slip st **loosely** in each st across ending in center ch of next corner; finish off.

Join strips in same manner, working a slip stitch in joined corner chs of Squares.

Placement Diagram

EDGING

Rnd 1: With **right** side facing, working in Front Loops Only and in joinings, join Purple with slip st in center ch of any corner ch-3; slip st in next st and in each st around; join with slip st to joining slip st, finish off.

Rnd 2: With **right** side facing, working **behind** previous rnd and in free loops of sts on each Square, join Ecru with dc in same st as joining; ch 3, dc in same st, ch 1, (skip next st, dc in next dc, ch 1) 17 times, skip next st, ★ † dc in same st as joining, ch 1, (skip next st, dc in next dc, ch 1) 17 times, skip next st †; repeat from † to † across to center ch of next corner ch-3, (dc, ch 3, dc) in center ch, ch 1, (skip next st, dc in next dc, ch 1) 17 times, skip next st; repeat from ★ 2 times **more**, then repeat from † to † across; join with slip st to first dc, do **not** finish off.

Rnd 3: Ch 4 **(counts as first dc plus ch 1)**, turn; working in both loops, skip next ch, ★ (dc in next dc, ch 1, skip next ch) across to center ch of next corner ch-3, (dc, ch 3, dc) in center ch, ch 1, skip next ch; repeat from ★ around; join with slip st to first dc, finish off.

Rnd 4: With **right** side facing and working in both loops, join Purple with sc in first ch in any corner ch-3; (2 sc, ch 1, 2 sc) in next ch, sc in next ch, ★ ch 1, skip next dc, (sc in next ch, ch 1, skip next dc) across to next corner ch-3, sc in next ch, (2 sc, ch 1, 2 sc) in center ch, sc in next ch; repeat from ★ 2 times **more**, ch 1, skip next dc, (sc in next ch, ch 1, skip next dc) across; join with slip st to first sc, finish off.

General INSTRUCTIONS

ABBREVIATIONS

ch(s)	chain(s)
cm	centimeters
dc	double crochet(s)
hdc	half double crochet(s)
mm	millimeters
Rnd(s)	Round(s)
sc	single crochet(s)
sp(s)	space(s)
st(s)	stitch(es)
tr	treble crochet(s)
YO	yarn over

★ — work instructions following ★ as many **more** times as indicated in addition to the first time.

† to † **or** ♥ to ♥ — work all instructions from first † to second † **or** first ♥ to second ♥ **as many** times as specified.

( ) or [ ] — work enclosed instructions **as many** times as specified by the number immediately following **or** work all enclosed instructions in the stitch or space indicated **or** contains explanatory remarks.

colon (:) — the number(s) given after a colon at the end of a row or round denote(s) the number of stitches you should have on that row or round.

CROCHET TERMINOLOGY		
UNITED STATES		INTERNATIONAL
slip stitch (slip st)	=	single crochet (sc)
single crochet (sc)	=	double crochet (dc)
half double crochet (hdc)	=	half treble crochet (htr)
double crochet (dc)	=	treble crochet(tr)
treble crochet (tr)	=	double treble crochet (dtr)
double treble crochet (dtr)	=	triple treble crochet (ttr)
triple treble crochet (tr tr)	=	quadruple treble crochet (qtr)
skip	=	miss

Yarn Weight Symbol & Names	LACE 0	SUPER FINE 1	FINE 2	LIGHT 3	MEDIUM 4	BULKY 5	SUPER BULKY 6
Type of Yarns in Category	Fingering, 10-count crochet thread	Sock, Fingering Baby	Sport, Baby	DK, Light Worsted	Worsted, Afghan, Aran	Chunky, Craft, Rug	Bulky, Roving
Crochet Gauge* Ranges in Single Crochet to 4" (10 cm)	32-42 double crochets**	21-32 sts	16-20 sts	12-17 sts	11-14 sts	8-11 sts	5-9 sts
Advised Hook Size Range	Steel*** 6,7,8 Regular hook B-1	B-1 to E-4	E-4 to 7	7 to I-9	I-9 to K-10.5	K-10.5 to M-13	M-13 and larger

*GUIDELINES ONLY: The chart above reflects the most commonly used gauges and hook sizes for specific yarn categories.

** Lace weight yarns are usually crocheted on larger-size hooks to create lacy openwork patterns. Accordingly, a gauge range is difficult to determine. Always follow the gauge stated in your pattern.

*** Steel crochet hooks are sized differently from regular hooks–the higher the number the smaller the hook, which is the reverse of regular hook sizing.

CROCHET HOOKS													
U.S.	B-1	C-2	D-3	E-4	F-5	G-6	H-8	I-9	J-10	K-10½	N	P	Q
Metric - mm	2.25	2.75	3.25	3.5	3.75	4	5	5.5	6	6.5	9	10	15

BEGINNER	Projects for first-time crocheters using basic stitches. Minimal shaping.
EASY	Projects using yarn with basic stitches, repetitive stitch patterns, simple color changes, and simple shaping and finishing.
INTERMEDIATE	Projects using a variety of techniques, such as basic lace patterns or color patterns, mid-level shaping and finishing.
EXPERIENCED	Projects with intricate stitch patterns, techniques and dimension, such as non-repeating patterns, multi-color techniques, fine threads, small hooks, detailed shaping and refined finishing.

GAUGE

Exact gauge is **essential** for proper size. Before beginning your project, make the sample swatch given in the individual instructions in the yarn and hook specified. After completing the swatch, measure it, counting your stitches and rows or rounds carefully. If your swatch is larger or smaller than specified, **make another, changing hook size to get the correct gauge**. Keep trying until you find the size hook that will give you the specified gauge.

JOINING WITH SC

When instructed to join with sc, begin with a slip knot on hook. Insert hook in stitch or space indicated, YO and pull up a loop, YO and draw through both loops on hook.

JOINING WITH HDC

When instructed to join with hdc, begin with a slip knot on hook. YO, holding loop on hook, insert hook in stitch or space indicated, YO and pull up a loop (3 loops on hook), YO and draw through all 3 loops on hook.

JOINING WITH DC

When instructed to join with dc, begin with a slip knot on hook. YO, holding loop on hook, insert hook in stitch or space indicated, YO and pull up a loop (3 loops on hook), (YO and draw through 2 loops on hook) twice.

BACK RIDGE

Work only in loops indicated by arrows ***(Fig. 1)***.

Fig. 1

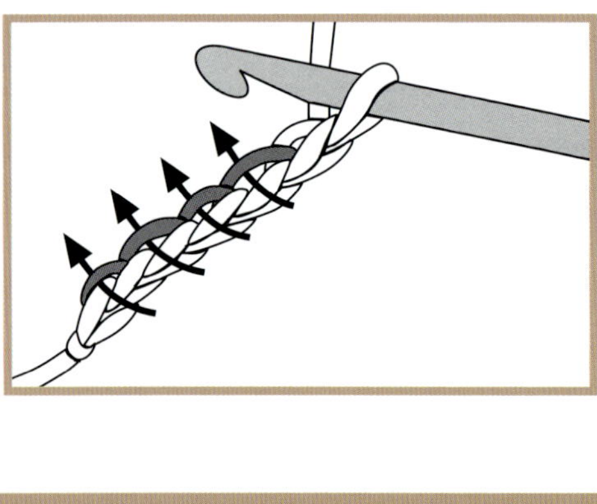

BACK OR FRONT LOOP ONLY

Work only in loop(s) indicated by arrow ***(Fig. 2a and b)***.

Fig. 2a

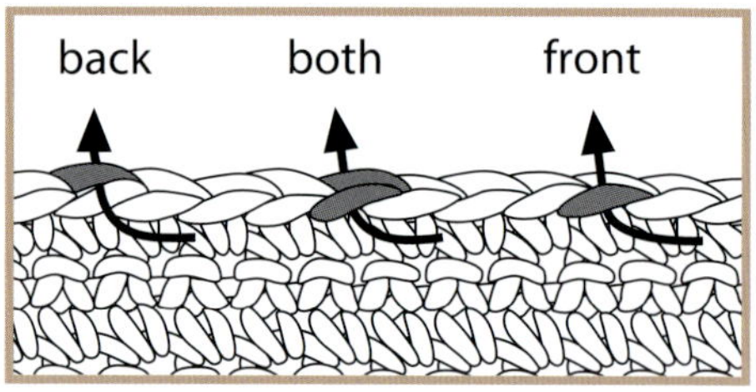

Fig. 2b

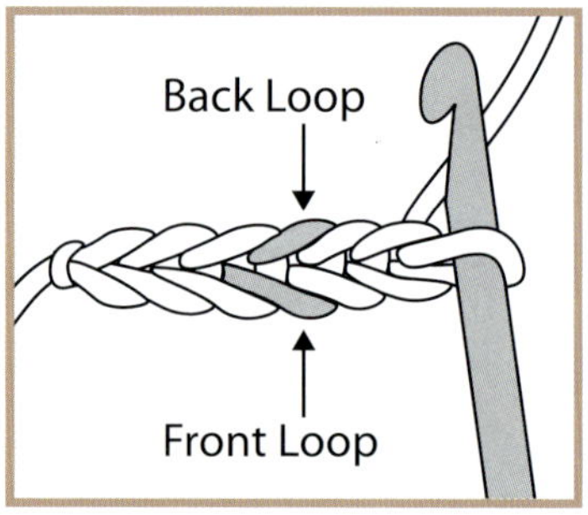

FREE LOOPS

After working in Back or Front Loops Only on a row or round, there will be a ridge of unused loops. These are called the free loops. Later, when instructed to work in the free loops of the same row or round, work in these loops ***(Fig. 3a)***.
When instructed to work in free loop of a chain, work in loop indicated by arrow ***(Fig. 3b or Fig. 3c)***.

Fig. 3a

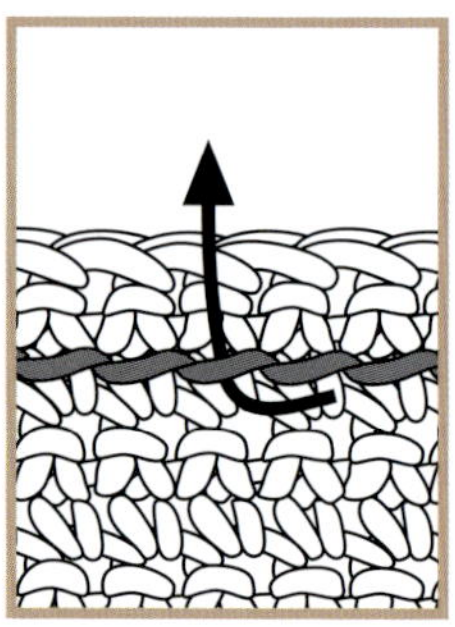

Fig. 3b

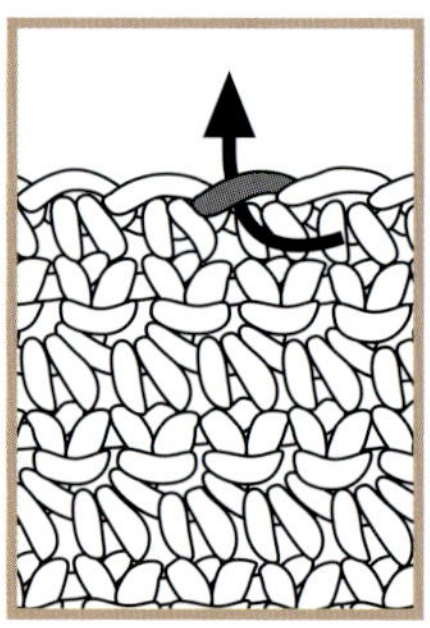

Fig. 3c

WORKING IN FRONT LEG AND IN WRAP OF STITCH

Insert hook in loops indicated by arrow ***(Fig. 4)***.

Fig. 4

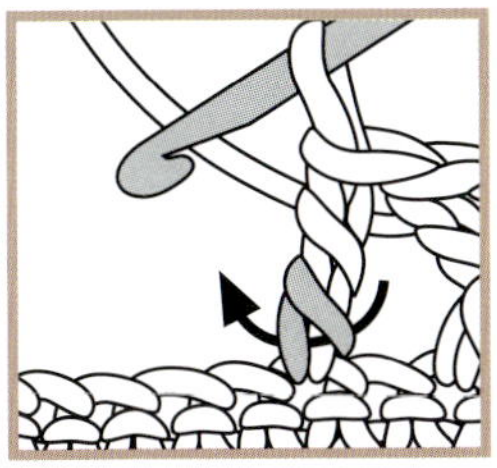

REVERSE SINGLE CROCHET

(abbreviated reverse sc)

Working from **left** to **right**, ★ insert hook in st to right of hook ***(Fig. 5a)***, YO and draw through, under and to left of loop on hook (2 loops on hook) ***(Fig. 5b)***, YO and draw through both loops on hook ***(Fig. 5c)*** **(reverse sc made, *Fig. 5d*)**; repeat from ★ around.

Fig. 5a

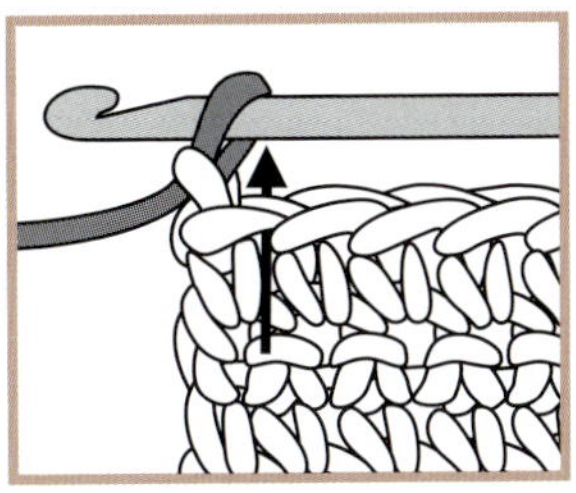

Fig. 5b

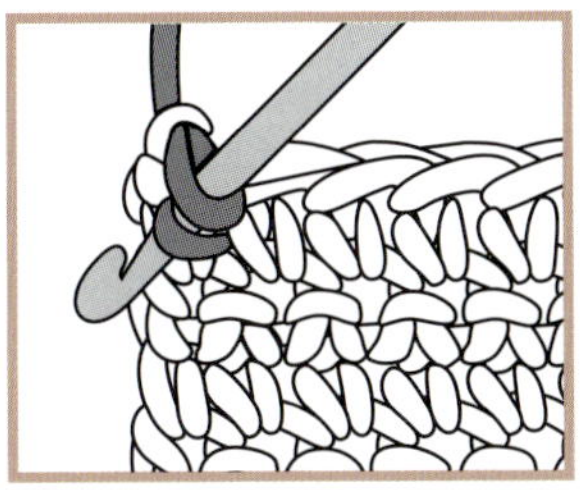

Fig. 5c

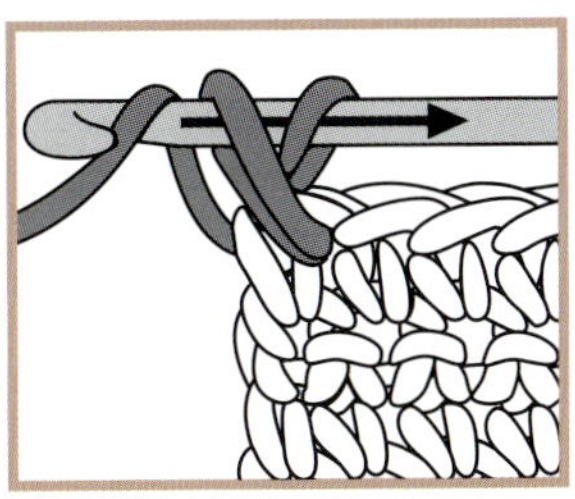

Fig. 5d

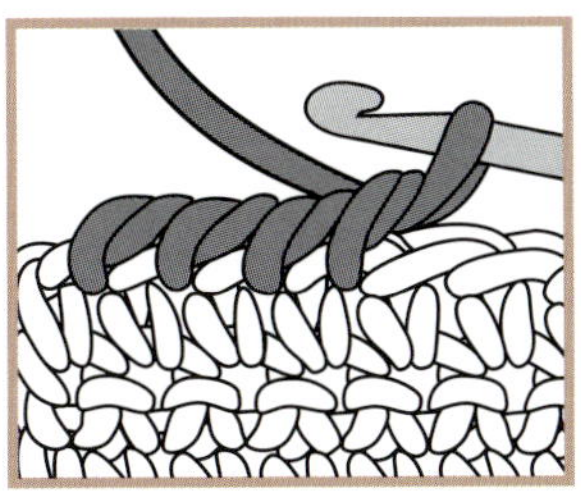

FRINGE

Cut a piece of cardboard 5" (12.5 cm) wide by 6" (15 cm) long. Wind the yarn **loosely** and **evenly** lengthwise around the cardboard until the card is filled, then cut across one end; repeat as needed. Hold together as many strands as specified in individual instructions; fold in half.

With **wrong** side facing and using a crochet hook, draw the folded end up through a space and pull the loose ends through the folded end ***(Fig. 6a)***; draw the knot up **tightly** ***(Fig. 6b)***.

Repeat, spacing as specified in individual instructions.

Lay flat on a hard surface and trim the ends.

Fig. 6a

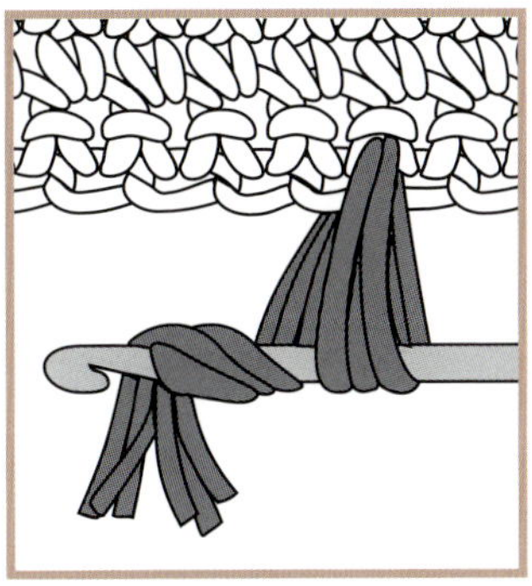

Fig. 6b

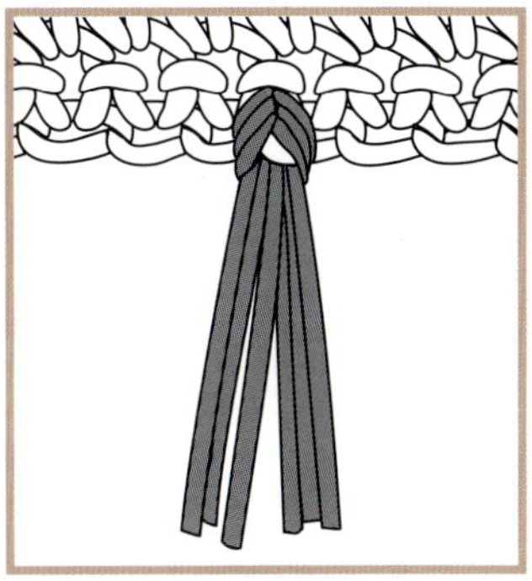

We have made every effort to ensure that these instructions are accurate and complete. We cannot, however, be responsible for human error, typographical mistakes, or variations in individual work.

Instructions tested and photo models made by Janet Akins, Marianna Crowder, Sue Galucki, and Raymelle Greening.

Production Team: Instructional Editor - Lois J. Long; Technical Editor - Sarah J. Green; Editorial Writer - Susan McManus Johnson; Senior Graphic Artist - Lora Puls; Graphic Artist - Dana Vaughn; Photo Stylist - Christy Myers; and Photographer - Ken West.

YARN INFORMATION

Each item in this leaflet was made with Medium Weight Yarn with the exception of the Garden Trellis which was made with Bulky Weight Yarn. Any brand of the specified yarn may be used. It is best to refer to the yardage/meters when determining how many balls or skeins to purchase. Remember, to arrive at the finished size, it is the GAUGE/TENSION that is important, not the brand of yarn.

For your convenience, listed below are yarns used to create our photography models.

ROSE PROMENADE

TLC® Essentials™

Off-White - #2316 Winter White
Rose - #2772 Lt Country Rose
Green - #2615 Lt Celery

CHRISTMAS BOUQUET

Red Heart® Super Saver®

Off-White - #316 Soft White
Red - #376 Burgundy
Green - #406 Medium Thyme
Yellow - #320 Cornmeal

SPICE GARDENS

Lion Brand® Vanna's Choice® Baby

Off-White - #098 Lamb
Yellow - #157 Duckie

Lion Brand® Vanna's Choice®

Orange - #134 Terracotta
Red - #133 Brick

GARDEN TRELLIS

Bernat® Softee® Chunky

Ecru - #39008 Natural
Blue - #39116 Denim Heather

TOWN SQUARE

Lion Brand® Wool-Ease®

Ecru - #99 Fisherman
Purple - #191 Violet
Green - #174 Avocado
Rust - #188 Paprika